IN THE CROSSHAIRS

An Anthology of Protest Poems and Prose

Compiled by Ayo Gutierrez & Bryan Oliphint
Edited by Tanya Mead
Cover by Emily St. Marie
Layout by Jinque Romanban-Dolojan

DISCLAIMER

The views expressed here are solely those of the authors and do not reflect the views of the publisher.

FOREWORD

Is this whole world burning down to hell?

Let's look at ourselves in a mirror—the reflection staring back at us won't be flattering. "Our species is facing moral poverty," claims Kelly Glover in her poem, "Who Will Know." It's hard to argue against that! Selfishness, greed, lack of empathy and compassion, corruption, violence, hatred . . . It's not only the West which is rotten (as Thomas Spychalski outlines in "Western World View"). Everywhere indeed the fat cats of a self-serving elite, which has never been richer, dine on "fifty-dollar steak" (Jai Thoolen, "My Frequent Flyer Miles") while the vast majority of humanity is just trying to get by and survive.

Anger and resentment have reached a boiling point among the have-nots. In these times of economic uncertainty and instability, how many have already completely bitten the dust to end up destitute? How many more are just walking that thin bread-line between having a roof above their heads and sleeping rough? Homelessness can strike blindly indeed, as Lena Power starkly reminds us in "Isolation on the Streets." But who cares? We don't even care about our own planet!

Agonized, raped, and plundered mercilessly, suffocating through destruction and climate change, our poor Earth is left to starve, crying out like a bleeding heart for compassion. "Revolving Extinction" by Kelly Glover and "Progress" by Tissy Taylor are powerful snapshots of it all; yet brace yourself! This isn't even the tip of the melting iceberg—or what's left of it, which is not much. Oh well! Let it melt. As M Lynn painfully notes in "Save the Planet?"—when it will flood us all shame will sustain us; if we haven't become extinct by then (Lena Power, "Last to Die")! But this won't matter either. After all, aren't we used to dabbling in shame by now? For isn't it what we want to teach to our kids? The world we want to leave them? Our legacy to future generations?

Our kids . . . Most of them are already growing up in poverty. Many are raised by struggling single mothers fighting to make ends meet with nothing to support them but misplaced guilt about their situations (Ayo Gutierrez, "V Monologue"). At least most don't have to go and sell themselves like some poor women, or men for that matter, end up doing ("Whore" by Ndotono Waweru, "Your Little Whore" by Jai Thoolen, "Charlie in Box" by Johnny Francis Wolf). So, what's to be done?

Try and escape? Resort to drugs, maybe—newfound addictions as toxic and pathetic as the reality surrounding us. "Overdose" by Kelly Glover, "The Cocaine Lost" by M Lynn . . . Wouldn't a shot in the head be better than such slow-death shots in the arms? Even better, what about playing the blame game? We search for scapegoats to blame for our misfortunes, for we have been told and preached to and brainwashed by our politicians ("nefarious ensemble / singing lies through sharp-toothed smiles" –Ayo Gutierrez, "Delicadeza"): our lot is not greed's fault or the result of political incompetence! No, no, no, our leaders assure us! It's the economy, stupid, they repeat with straight faces. Or, it's the fault of others. Strangers. Immigrants daring to beg for their part of a dream, while here I am reading "Pen of Wise Pigs" by Edentu Oroso and smiling a wry smile. Fools!

Isn't it ironic that on the one hand, some fat-crass Westerners fed on porn wouldn't mind flying across the globe to go and exploit certain foreigners, even in the most debasing way ("Fields Avenue" by Ayo Gutierrez says it all), yet on the other hand, they will passionately refuse others asylum when they come knocking at their doors as refugees? Wall them out, they preach! Walls always solve problems; from Berlin to Gaza, it's a well-known historical fact, isn't? Ha! But they're not white, are they?

History . . . Birmingham, 1963. Charlottesville, 2018. Images of violence, hatred, and sickening racism fill our screens to the point of vomit. Just read "Vanilla" by Kelly Glover . . . and God Bless America! Or maybe not. Maybe God can't bless anything anymore. Maybe He is too busy gambling our Faustian lot with the Devil? Or is He the Devil himself? Does He even deserve his name to be capitalised (Kelly Glover, "god Not Capitalized")? Violence and bigotry are still a brutal and sickening reality for some ("Verdict" by Ayo Gutierrez), and God is in bad shape to come and rescue us. Don't pray too much. Instead, just barricade yourselves in the comfort of your houses. Safe. Secure. Cosy.

Or are they? Ask those wives awaiting new bruises to come through the door (Johnny Francis Wolf, "Narrative (With Caveats)"). Ask those children awaiting new abuses to come through the door (Lena Power,

"Daddy"). Ask all of them, in fact, and see how many are out there "living on stolen childhood" ("Succumb" by Ndotono Waweru)! And how much longer is this tragedy going to go on? Like a dog returning to its vomit, the cycle seems never-ending (Kelly Glover, "Prisoners").

Alas, we carry on, but not like soldiers on battlefields. No, for there is no glory in wars, as Ndotono Waweru reminds us in "A General's Mirror." What are wars, anyway? Pete Cox tells us: "War is business / People are the currency/ . . . Spray it over the news / . . . Then sell us remembrance." War, in an age of deafness to history and paranoiac fears, is indeed just that: another hypocrisy. We don't even respect our veterans anymore (M Lynn, "Stereo Typical")! No, we carry on though we feel like shutting off. Depressing, isn't it?

In "Unwanted," M Lynn echoes this profound hopelessness: "Choking on life's stagnant bile / Reaching out into emptiness / Comfort in abysmal darkness / Just a fucking nothing and unwanted." The world is suffocating. The paranoia, insecurity, anxiety, turmoil, loneliness, worthlessness, and hopelessness of it all just pushes us against a wall. Fight or flight? Neither. Just break down. After all, aren't we all somewhat similar to the main character in "Liberty" by Simon Jackson: patronized, but rowing on? Sure, we may be sedated; glued as we are to our screens and triumphant individualism, but gosh! How entertained are we?! Who can even blame us for our complacent passivity?

So here we are. Is this whole world burning down to hell? I don't know— but if it's true that we are going down in flames, then setting things ablaze further couldn't do much harm.

Aurélien Thomas is a poet who lives in London, England. He is currently working on *A Vow*, a whimsy collection of love poems ranging from the romantically sweet to the boldly erotic. *A Vow* is due for publication soon, although some extracts have already appeared in various international publications.

CONTRIBUTORS

Pete Cox
Kelly Glover
Ayo Gutierrez
Simon Jackson
M Lynn
Edentu Oroso
Lena Power
Thomas Spychalski
Tissy Taylor
Jai Thoolen
Ndotono Waweru
Johnny Francis Wolf

REVIEWS

These writers draw a bead on the most hypocritical behavior of our time. You will find them erudite and not afraid to speak the truth. It is hard to put this anthology down. The writers represent some of the top writing talent out there. Their awards and acknowledgements pile high. The words are powerful. The assessments real. The hopes sincere.

— David Wagoner, Author of *Scratches & Scraps*

If you feel things are worse than usual, if you are horrified by open racism, and if you are ready to hear something that makes sense instead of just doublespeak slogans, this is the book for you. These talented writers catch the issues of the day "In The Crosshairs."

— Sharon Wagoner, Author of *The Inheritance*

In the Crosshairs is a cry from the point of view of the downtrodden. It is a mirror held up to the face of society, a bellowing call to attention to everything that is wrong with our world today. It is a slap in the face for those who are still sleepwalking, and it's timely at that.

— Benoit Chartier, Author of *Red Nexus* and *Afterdeath*

It's no secret that changing times, economic strife, political upheaval, and social problems both big and small (if there is such a thing) are invariably reflected in art, in particular the written word. It's all part of the human condition; how we process and come to terms with what happens to and around us. We live in a challenging climate, and this anthology featuring some of the finest up-and-coming poets from around the world captures the very essence of what it means to be a citizen of the world. The conflict, the uncertainty, the greed, the soulnessness, the visceral urge to document the dark underbelly of society as mankind plots its own demise and through it all, that solitary undying flame of hope leading the way to a better future which could be our only salvation.

—C.M. Saunders, Journalist and Author of *Sker House, Dead of Night, X: Omnibus,* and other work

CONTENTS

1	**Social Injustices**	1
2	**Crimes Against Nature**	23
3	**Mental Health**	30
4	**Abuse**	44
5	**Religion**	62
6	**Revolution, Violence, and War**	86
7	**Oppressive Family Traditions**	91
7	**Politics**	98
8	**Open Themes**	114

SOCIAL INJUSTICES

Fire Wheel

By Thomas Spychalski

Black and white, no room for gray,
There is hatred in every word you say.
Closed mind, unhealed hearts,
Only freeze the world, shattered ice,
The fire of ignorance has become your vice.
Listen up and listen well,
To these words, I spit.
Pay attention this is your intervention,
That makes the world of one split,
Turning heavens to hells.

False self-respect, something you inject,
Into every rant and raving desire,
No room to introspect, just reject,
Why keep fueling the wheel of fire?

Cannot you see your brothers and sisters,
The ones you kill in your arms willingly,
Too ignorantly proud, way too vapidly loud,
Keep that burning wheel turning, so chillingly.

Shut your fucking mouth if you don't understand,
What it means to be a strong woman, a stand-up man.
Take your lumps this is life we learn from pain,
No lesson ever in labels and passing the blame.

One last section, my vision is clear as morning dew,
Before you ask someone else, what is wrong with you?
Hyper typing, media sheep biting, constantly blighting,
The things they never want us to see are true . . .
. . . we are the same, no shame, misplaced blame,
Push that broken wheel, it turns because of you.

BLOCK

By Johnny Francis Wolf

::: :::

Whack-A-Mole our rainbow globe,
vales and summits frame . . .

Those who, missing frontal lobe,
humans, but in name.

::: :::

Efforts made to paint us gray,
brushes dripping bleach . . .

You and I will slip away,
of color, we will teach.

::: :::

Blending shades of painted flags,
chroma spreading truth . . .

Bleeding red, the banner sags,
fixed at voting booth.

- - -
By Pete Cox

The daily cash rape queue formulates to pay the council tax
slavery
The sheriff is scouting around town
Corruption holds a crown over the already debt drowned
There's a look of disdain
Made from a government formula of pain-bound chains
We all don't say "fuck this, carry on, it's time to burn down
Babylon"
Instead we stew in the soup of how to conform since you
were born
Well, I'm getting warm
A hood-robbing hood is chopping wood to burn the no-good
tricks of a matrix pill found quest, that's opening the chest of
how to invest in making a mess with the powers that try to
test
Quite an itch
In the life of bitch
Time to tax the rich

Something missing

By Johnny Francis Wolf

===

I could give a flying f_ _k
What others think of me

Let them mire in the muck,
stuck, forever be.

===

Wild eyes with daggers shout,
angry words come through.

Stop the madness, turn about . . .
I look the same as you.

===

Broken bridges, sinking ships,
dirigibles on fire.

Weathered parchment, full of rips,
balanced on a wire.

===

Shared . . . the fate of every man,
fragile skin and bone.

Mend the heart, the bridge's span . . .
we are not alone.

===

Patch the soul, fake a grin,
reinforce the mesh.

Still the ire lives within,
extracts its pound of flesh.

Cuttings

By Thomas Spychalski

Clipped like a bird which cannot fly,
Torched like ancient standing people,
Dug into for treasure now barren,
This is how she will pass away.

Machinations breathe out fiery smoke,
Death coming in fruitless choking gasps,
Health depleted by doses of self-poison,
This is how we do our mother so proud.

Cuttings of our only home,
Lay on now barren ground,
Blindfolded, we march on,
Her children will be the ones to go.

Hunted like rare trophies of pride,
Carcasses only skeletons remain.
Farmed into an endless production,
That is how they vanished away.

Awaken we try but find no morning,
While business is the only order today,
Committing future genocide in passing,
No one stops the wheel's spin in symbiosis.

Cuttings of our future family taken,
Lay dormant due to obtuse muses,
Brake now or hold your silence on,
Our world will be the casualty of greed.

Vanilla

By Kelly Glover

Vanilla is the most boring of all flavors
It needs to be French, or drizzled with caramel
Chocolate or rainbow sprinkles to be fun
What is white is not always what is right

Chalky mold on a diseased leaf
Infecting a plant through its own wounds
What is white is not always what is right

Ivory Oleander an exquisite killer
The same shades of Hemlock, Poppy, and Hellebore
All gorgeous poisons

Cocaine nose candy disrupting lives
There is no reading between those snorted lines
What is white is not always what is right

Frosty ice crystals
Feasting on freezer-burnt raw meat
Lost in the back of your Frigidaire

Ravenous maggots feeding at the dinner table
The child of a fly that eats you when you die
What is white is not always what is right

The White House and its inhabitant
Now with the ugliest interior on the block
Casting deep shadows on our nation

Hooded Nazis and their supremist confederate counterparts
Projecting hate by magnifying race
What is white is not always what is right

Isolation on the Streets

By Lena Power

I s this my life now
S hattered and torn apart
O n my own to die?
L iving is so hard
A bandoned, tears falling
T ossed out to starve
I had my own home
O nly I fell on hard times
N ever to arise
O nce I had hot food
N ice warm sheets in which to sleep
T hen I lost control
H ow do I survive
E ndure humiliation
S tarving and so cold?
T aken all my things
R esistance is so futile
E ver left begging
E ven thieves get food
T he politicians hold rule
S ocial standing.

Who Will Know?

By Kelly Glover

For richer or poorer
As it is written in vows
The former promises to lift the latter up the ladder
Wealth is not all that matters

A tattered Gypsy's plea for recognition
Kneeling on the sidewalk
Arms stretched across the walkway
Blocking everyone's path
Forcing people to step over
Humanity
The day disappears, as does she
Back to a commune
Nicer than what's bought with minimum wage

The richest elite claim tax cuts
Help the working class poorest, but
Every fight ever won, every law ever done
Benefits only the very top ones
Wolves pulling the wool over sheep's eyes
Who will know?

Big Pharma, Big Insurance
One makes unaffordable drugs
While the other refuses to pay for them
Chronic disease infests the system
Dangling medication out of reach to the sick
That can save
Insurance instead pays for the drugs
That can euthanize
Compassionate dying

Thousands of dollars in credit card debt
Leaves us underwater searching for gold
The more they sell, the more we buy

With money that never existed
Buy now, pay later
But later never pays
It even costs to file bankruptcy
Pay to say you have nothing to pay

We give to beggars for the sake of humanity
Humanely give spare change for drugs
Each dollar closer to the next bottle
How must it feel to ask for money on a train?
Or hold a sign on the corner
Until there's enough money for a sack of cocaine?
Who will know?

Our species is facing moral poverty
Human beings are more than broke
Taking loans out on all the lies
The bank closed for most
Safe cracked for just a few
The poor have the richest attributes
The rich the poorest attitudes

Stereo Typical

By M Lynn

I see you over there
   Trying hard not to stare
I see your judgment all over your face
   Thinking the likes of me doesn't belong in this place
I see your nose turn up in disgust
   Scanning my appearance with eyes full of distrust
I wear my boots over my tucked-in jeans
   You laugh because you don't understand what it means
I see my scars and tattoos as art; some stories only need ink
   Not dirty or disgusting . . . Not that I care what you think
I see your smirk
   And think you're a jerk
I see your rights are exactly the same as mine
   As a military veteran, a better friend . . . you'll surely never find
I see my life in reverse; my regrets are ZERO
   Most people hear of my past service and even call me a hero
But I still see you sitting over there
   UNSEEING in your little judging mental chair

Chaos

By Lena Power

From the downfall of Adam and Eve
Who dared to eat of the fruit of knowledge
Social injustice is to be perceived
Inequality has to be acknowledged
Born equal, of the same flesh and blood
Ever were inequalities devised
Hatred erupted from the white man's hood
All different from them were despised
The feminine ever cursed, berated
Lowered to a second-class standing
Mankind became divided, separated
The upper echelons ever demanding
Dare you seek to love one of the same gender
Because that was your natural inclination
Or to become a cursed gender bender
You were surely headed for damnation

Irish were good to hire for cheap labour
The lower classes to be held in service
A serving wench certainly no stranger
To the higher class's secret preference
Division of riches is laughed upon
Food not needed kept from the poor
Education depends on where you're born
Hypocrisy is now the social norm
So let us talk about social injustice
It is prevalent throughout this world
A ten-year-old child sold into marriage
An elderly pensioner left to die of cold
Children denied proper education
Forsaken to a life of pure slavery
Soldiers surviving battlefield cremation
Left to insanity for their bravery
The homeless, the beggars on the streets
Most oft for no fault of their own making

SOCIAL INJUSTICES

Empty eyes of their despondency speak
While the world turns away, humanity forsaking

Politicians paid thousands to spew lies
Seeking only to line their own pockets
While every day hundreds more die
With pain pouring from their eye sockets.

By Pete Cox

A curious mutant enters a room
Sent by the abacus of doom
Scared eyes scout for pulses
Sniffing frequencies
The scent of fear is impulsive
Frosted skin blisters the chosen
The abattoir of existence is always open
I watch the dance of death dealers
Trying to stop them was a painful teacher
I've shaken hands with these creatures
I carry their mark
They gave me a gift
Followed by a devilish laugh
They circle me like chum
Believing I am theirs I see all their movement
For I am the accountant
I hide in plain sight
I humour their game
I hold my ace card tight

This Me

By Tissy Taylor

Colour me naked
All of me exposed
Liquid hate spilling
Tearing flesh from bone

Heavy rains falling
Forged river from fear
Shadow my disguise
Quiet lonely tears

Savage the beastly
Sheep who crowd the King
Red beats in anger
Evil from within

Adrift she is lost
Beckoned from beneath
Soothing deep waters
From your blade unsheathed

Crimson my rainbow
Quell the world above
Flow the ebbing tide
Seeking only love

Bright Eyes
By Tissy Taylor

Bright eyes crystallized
Beggars' night respite
Feather wishes fly
Silver lining heights

Golden dreams of mine
Fairy dust replete
Coral castle clouds
Happiness supreme

A scoop of Heaven
Kept inside a jar
Should I feel lonely
Alone in my heart

The mean things they say
Hurtful stuff they do
All my bumps and bruises
Break my soul in two

Mama says, "I love you"
Sorry for what she did
Daddy didn't mean to
You need to be good

Far away, high up
Castle in my mind
I am a Princess
Everyone is kind

Where Mommies give kisses
And Daddies never hit
Candy corn for breakfast
A life that is perfect

Bright eyes, crystallized

Tears from Heaven fall
My jar is empty
No happy left—at all!

My Frequent Flyer Miles

By Jai Thoolen

I eat my fifty-dollar steak.
I drink expensive wine.
Complain that everything is poor,
When really it is fine.
I tip the minimum amount.
I do not smile or thank.
I look down on the workers.
They're well below my rank.
I drive a Maserati.
I'm better than most folk.
MY house has thirteen bedrooms.
These people are all broke!
I fly to third world countries,
On my frequent flyer miles.
I tour around and laugh at folk,
Who've not eaten in a while.
I stay in five-star hotels.
I'm treated like a king,
And all these broken families,
Can hardly do a thing.
Why should I help degenerates,
Who haven't got a job?
I'm far too rich to give a shit!
I'd rather be a snob.
I don't want to catch something,
Or touch the filthy swine.
I'll keep eating fifty-dollar steaks,
And drinking fancy wine . . .

Liberty

By Simon Jackson

"Liberty," he repeated, stone-faced. He placed his coffee on his desk and leaned back, scrutinising me over his spectacles. With a faint sneer, he whispered, "Liberty?"

He eased out of his chair and slipped his hands into his pockets. "I wonder if you really know the meaning?" He turned towards the window and looked out.

"In truth I'm glad you came to see me," he turned and smiled briefly, "Because I think it's difficult, in the short life of just one man, to really see things like this with the necessary, err, historical perspective." He paused, satisfied at the effect of his introduction, until he saw my confusion and sighed.

"So, do you read books?" I shook my head. "No? Well, never mind. I read a bit, mostly novels, but also anthropology. You know, origins of man, prehistory stuff. And so, I sometimes ask myself, what did our distant ancestor have in his life, besides the merciless toil of his brief existence?

"Not for Cro-Magnon man were the comforts of modern life. No weekends with his girlfriend in the Algarve. No Instagram update of a white-washed fishing village. No air-conditioned hire-car. No filter cigarettes. No fast-food, well, except that it ran fast." He chuckled at his quip.

"I'll tell you what he had. He had such awful danger visit him in the dead of night that to this very day, men are genetically predisposed to sleep nearer to the entrance of their homes than their female partners. How many generations do you think it took, of fathers fighting off wolves in the night, to instil that habit in the male psyche? How many lost children?"

He returned to the table. "How would you like it, to live in a world where another man can step forward and take your woman, for no other reason than he's bigger and tougher than you, and he'll kill you if you try to stop him?"

"Even as recently as the 1850s, forty-five percent of children died before their fifth birthdays. Disease, accidents, genetics, killed half of all the people who'd ever lived. To parents like you and I, it's an appalling idea, but that's how it was. People died all the time." He shrugged.

"So, what did ancient man do in the face of this unrelenting despair?" He leaned over the table and jabbed it with his finger as he spoke. "I'll tell you, he learned to cooperate. He learned to give up some of his own interests, his own wealth, his own time. He learned to give just a little bit to the group. And in doing so he gained so much more in return. Sure, competition has played its part in the evolution of man: one man catches more fish than the next, and so his family prospers. But one man can't be good at everything. By cooperating, each man does what he's best at, and everyone succeeds.

"No doubt it was a struggle to give up old feuds and make friends with old enemies, and I'm sure there were some who didn't care to cooperate." He undid the buttons of his jacket to air his shirt. I glimpsed the worn pistol attached to his belt. "Thankfully, common sense prevailed."

He dropped into his chair and finished his coffee. "And then, our ancestor was no longer a slave to nature. He gained his freedom from the misery and death, he'd won his Liberty. Liberty for you and I, our children, their children yet to be born. We owe a great deal to the people of our past; because of them, every one of us is born free."

He folded his hands in his lap. I saw the image of my two girls, safe and warm, breathing softly under their bed-clothes.

I felt his eyes upon me, and we sat in silence. At last, he let out a breath and spoke quietly, "Alright then."

He looked at his watch and smiled, "Well, as I said, I'm glad you came to see me." He walked around the table and extended his hand. I shook it, placing my untouched coffee on the desk, and he led me to the door. "I'll take you back down."

A sea breeze swept in and I followed him along the passageway, onto the deck. No sooner had my eyes adjusted to the bright blue horizon than he lifted a hatch and held it open for me.

As we made our way deeper into the ship, I heard the drum, and the creak of the oars, and felt pangs of excitement.

When we reached the rowing deck, the sweat of one-hundred-and-thirteen men hung in the air and soaked into the deck and the bulkheads. We walked along the gangway and a mist of seawater blew over the rail and cooled the crew as they set to their oars. Half-naked and swarthy, three rows deep on each side, every man held his own oar and matched the stroke as one, moving like a single, giant muscle.

The chief spied us and his drum signaled all-stop. The muscle relaxed.

Around the midships, I clambered on to my bench. Men positioned above me pulled my oar from the overhead compartment and threaded it over the rail.

One of the chief's crew came with a hammer and block and set about refitting my leg shackle. The captain laid a hand on his shoulder and shook his head. The chief's man shrugged and slipped away with my ankle-iron.

I gripped the indents in my oar and felt the contours in the deck planks from the sliding of my feet—memories of three years, and five-thousand nautical miles, worn into the wood.

The crew resumed their positions and the captain leaned towards me, "Tell me, what is it that you do best?" I held up my oar with both calloused hands. He smiled and laid his hand on my shoulder. He called out, "Carry on, Chief," and turned on his heel. I shouted after him, "Thank you, Captain," and he waved his acknowledgement.

The drummer signaled to ready the stroke. I stretched my shoulders and prepared to pull.

I Can't Breathe

By Ndotono Waweru

The tide has ebbed.
Back to the sea that cast her.
Buoyed through boulevards of anger.
And I still can't breathe.
Gulls have taken to the sky.
Chanting a worn-out prophecy
To culture-proofed ears.
And I still can't breathe.
Farmers of words enjoying a bounty.
Washed and rinsed by dirty tongues.
The symphony of a giddy justice.
And I still can't breathe.
Ants minding their orange moundhill.
Seekers of a young cure
To an old ailment.
And I still can't breathe.
Dealers of freedom in halls of justice.
Trimming bushes of humanity
For a pound of flesh.
And I still can't breathe.
The blueberries are still blue.
The blue jay still sings,
Of his wings and eggs that matter.
And I still can't breathe.

CRIMES AGAINST NATURE

Revolving Extinction

By Kelly Glover

Humans have forced extinct
Much more than they have created
Tusks and animal hides
Treasured as the golden prize

Elephants and rhinos
Will join the Dodo and the Mammoth
The only remnants ivory and horns
Made into aphrodisiacs to assist with porn

Poaching is murder
Extinction is revolving
Maybe one day it will be our teeth
Our hides hunted for meat

Anguished Cry

By Lena Power

Thunder roars, lightning strikes
Bees are dead, day is now night
Oceans polluted, fish are dying
Can you hear the weeping willows crying?

All the trees have been cut down
Not enough oxygen to go round
Babies crying while mothers wail
Searching for clean water, to no avail

Mother nature has been raped
It is a crime, make no mistake
She screams out her anguished cry
As man's pillage causes her to die

Mother Earth has finally had enough
Boiling with anger, volcanoes erupt
Spewing forth their intense fury
Seeking humanity to burn, to bury

Animals are dying by the second
Radioactivity has become fecund
Skeleton bones adorn the pavements
Our greed out of control, time for payment

Bare, so barren, Earth's treasures taken
Feeling unloved, completely forsaken
Wishing for a more evolved species
Who realise all life forms need to live

That means the birds, flowers, trees
The tiny ant, magnificent honey bees
Animals of all forms, all description
Control of nature is not man's jurisdiction.

Progress
By Tissy Taylor

Silver blades of wilted green
Lazy 'neath the blazing sun
Amid the blooming dahlias
Rest the whippoorwill, as she sings

Glass and steel to cinder meet
Escape the jungle's city street
Reach to heaven lest I breathe
Lonely willow empty reach

Great machines to keep us down
Building new from barren ground
Tearing flesh from broken soil
Rape and plunder, we will toil

Mighty mountains, icy steel
Unheeded, do as they please
Spoiled acres erased from Earth
Borrowed breaths 'til He renews

In the beginning there was
Lush greens founded by our God
So that we may live as one
In Man's shadow we will fall

God save us all

Last to Die

By Lena Power

I visit the ocean's shores
Reminiscing of a time when
I swam safely in her waters
Now to do so means poison

I visit the valleys of my youth
When all was green, so verdant
Now all I see is barren soil
Once majestic trees lying dead

Peering intently into the sky
Hoping to see birds flying
All I see are blackened clouds
The ozone layer still dying

Fervently my eyes gaze around
Looking for the source of silence
Seeing a haze of dusty fragments
Feeling the stillness of violence

There is no sign of movement
No pretty flowers for final joy
As the skin peels from my bones
I know I am the last to die.

Save The Planet?

By M Lynn

Humanity is lost and has forgotten the reason we are here
Senseless destruction of nature that was given to us with
a love sincere
Lands destroyed for buildings that will end vacant to rot and
decay
Forests gone with no thought to the air we breathe; humanity
gone
astray
Needless killings of animals just to sport trophies with no
intention to
feed
The circle of life is broken, and death is the new breed
Evolution has become our pollution and humanity deserves
no
litigation
So much disregard, greed, and immorality; we must kill this
damn
infestation
Destruction is insanity
Shame . . . Shame on our humanity

Boxes and cinder

By Tissy Taylor

Concrete walls push further
Defining city wealth
Glass ceilings to ponder
Building up. Building out

A single blade of grass
Resilient in his fate
Artificial turf war
Politicians placate

Boxes and cinder
Everyone looks the same
Satisfy the masses
Playing a losing game

Nature's revolution
Progression kills our soul
Sacred the grounds buried
Neath the mortar and stone

Where have the flowers gone?
Shy the growth in shadow
Stolen beauty we march
Her grasp, torn asunder

MENTAL HEALTH

The Bread Aisle

By Kelly Glover

Sitting in the parking lot
Gathering the courage
To exit safety
To enter awkwardness
Check the list
Check keys
Check phone
Check, Check, Check

Go. No more procrastinating
The key fob
Sounds a toot of security
A boost of confidence
To get in the store
Hurry up

Nervous eyes behind sunglasses hide
Removal leaves a target on my face
A shopping cart, metal comfort
I can put my hands on
As I try to ground

Rapid gasps suffocate
In the bread aisle
All know
All see
All care
All, All, All
Imminent embarrassment
The brainy fuzz doesn't allow for
Coherent thoughts
Instead it darkens
Sprinkled with dreamy delirium
Hang my head
No eye contact
Avoiding obligatory pleasantries

Look to the cans of condensed milk
For conversation

They demand no response
It is fight or flight
Hurry up

Unjust angst
Attention on my list
If attention to me is paid
They watch as I pick out zucchini
They watch as I weigh my apples
They watch the unhealthy purchases
Watch, Watch, Watch
Hurry up

A familiar face leads to twice as much anxiety
Always remain undetected
I hide from old boyfriends
I hide from old teachers
I hide from acquaintances
Hide, Hide, Hide

No backtracking
If something from the list is missed
It is abandoned until next time
Can't go down the bread aisle twice
Time to go
Hurry up

Pick the longest line to give more time
To prepare for interaction
Pretend to read *Time*
The person in front chats up the cashier
Sorts coupons
Counts coins
Makes me want to screech
Run wildly from the building
Finally my turn

Fidgeting until it's time to pay
Swiping a card
So no hand-to-hand contact
A rushed thank you

A rushed exit
A rushed return to the car
Rush, Rush, Rush

The bags are in the trunk
Cart returned
In the front seat
Freedom smells like
A puff of green anxiety meds
Until we meet again
Bread aisle

Doting Dolly

By Ndotono Waweru

Her face unfurls spring.
Nostalgia tucked beneath
her furrowed brow.
Her sight has found eternity
But her eyes still twinkle
In the arena of time.

Today,
She fell into
The inferno.

Walls moved and made her cry.
I was her thankless son
At lunch time.
A thief when
she couldn't find her dentures.
Now,
I am the sweetest nurse
That ever lived.

Tomorrow,
She will be a portrait
On the wall.
Her elegant smile
A balm to the
Passage of time.

War-Bride

By Thomas Spychalski

Called from memory,
Flashes incendiary.
Endless nameless dying,
Dried dead tears crying.

Miss my maternal maker,
Driven by inner undertaker,
I don't desire the silent curse,
So stained costumes we rehearse.

Can the skies show me some mercy?
I tried to glue this world so whole,
Doing out what cannot within, reverse,
Old wiring shows me who controls.

Can someone fix my outdated wires and leads,
Adjust my fears, navigate, control my speed,
The leash pulls my neck like an old unwanted friend,
See glimpses of my sanity in my heart now and then.

Somewhere between the crossed wires a good man died,
Out there in the cold world so many prophets have lied,
It's me and me and we always stand so far apart, yet aside,
Dark negative one, you are my cheating love, my war-bride.

Unwanted

By M Lynn

Tired of being a Nothing
Just wanna be somebody's something
Appreciated for my worth
Full of good lovin' to make others happy
Feelings say I'll never be that
Just depreciated value

No one to share life with
Or enjoy all its many pleasures
Destined to be alone
Being a Nothing begets misery
Heartaches and
Breaks at the thought
Of being unwanted

Hard to breathe
Swallow the lump in my throat
Choking on life's stagnant bile
Reaching out into emptiness
Comfort in abysmal darkness
Just a fucking Nothing and unwanted

Slate

By Ndotono Waweru

Sometimes I escape.
Back into my mind's scope.
Rummaging for forgotten hopes.
Visiting the past and all her slopes.

Hidden beyond this wrought-iron fate.
Tucked away behind a toddler gate.
Memories mired in fake spoils.
A voyage worth the toil.

Ruins mine to peek.
Further beyond errant creeks.
Decoding these mysterious clowns.
Trapped in a page, left in a golden town.

This olden library in my mind I browse,
Eager to venture, bygones roused.
Back here to petition my fate.
To demand a clean slate.

Mockingbird

By Lena Power

Shattered reality
Broken shards
All I see
Fragments of my mind
Obscure memories
I left behind
Mind torn apart
Sanity walked
Bleeding heart
Shadows haunting
Flesh torn
Demons taunting
Soul is shred
No light left
Fate is read
Haggard reflection
Stares in emptiness
Lost direction
No mercy left
Blood poisoned
Agony my theft
Dismal days
Spent in darkness
Lost my way
Can't be reached
Can't be helped
Please don't preach
Sing your song
Sweet Mockingbird
Everything is wrong
See you on
The other side
All hope now gone.

Comfortably Depressed

By Kelly Glover

Depression is my home sweet home
My worst emotional syndrome
It is safe and warm in the dark
Snuggled up under cover of night, no spark

Depression is a need
That one must acknowledge to set free
Like a cheating lover that dishonors and lies
Still you want more, desperate, it gets you high

Blissful as a suicide jump
Ignorant as a man named Trump
Depression has no permission
Favoring darkness like a mortician

I was born pink innocent and fresh
Not yet a bruise on this heart's flesh
The gray crept in and before I could stop it
The black pushed me headfirst into its pit

My color is purple now
Depression has finally taken a bow
It only feeds on what I allow
I starved it and pushed it out somehow

Depression was my friend
But I don't miss that guy
I put it to an end
Don't know where exactly it went
I just know I'll probably see it ag

Falling into Madness

By Lena Power

These images are surging all around
There's not a single letter to be found
I've lost count of their endless swirls
The incessant morphing is quite absurd
Floating into the vastness of space
Far away from this suffocating place
Mind is numb, senses are relapsing
Seems as if my universe is collapsing
What are those shining images I see
Could they be Angelic hosts calling to me?
Ever do they keep on drifting nearer
Though I've never been an avid believer
Falling down into the darkness of despair
Scrambling for a foothold, not one there
Tumbling into the realms of insanity
Screaming out loudly my agonised plea

Walls of my mind are ever closing in
Where does sanity end, madness begin?
My whole world in shambled destruction
Suicidal impulses my final instruction
How I long to exist in peacefulness
To a lifetime of sins I have confessed
Though by those I hurt I've been forgiven
Still never of this pain inside am I ridden.

Who Minds?

By Tissy Taylor

Silent screams vanished inside her head
Ghosts living within
Forgive me my sins
Bound she lay writhing soaked in madness
Wrists raw and bloodied
Sanctioned her silence
Of brick and mortar imprisoned mind
She has no voice
Little lamb bleating
Wretched soul, broken and bleeding
Begging her freedom
Sacrificed meaning
Unwilling descent, crawling demons
Stolen eyes watching
Grant me your false peace
He climbs atop her in dark of night
Ordained this evil
Blue pill and red pill
Pictures rain heavy against shut lids
Swallow my forked tongue
Green manicured lawn
A few tithes bestow the collection
Severed from his church
Deliver me please
Smooth the fraying hem, my butchers gown
Mind buried, useless
Who barters for me
Semen rooted from his greed planted
Takes all left of me
Left in fantasy
Skin and bones don't make me who I am
Will someone help me
I am nobody
Vessel of God abused and diseased
Void and empty she
Bloody her mercy

Who Am I?

By Tissy Taylor

Who do you want to be?
Do you have room for me?
Are you sweet
Kind and true
Angry or
Wanton
Happy, blue?
Pieces of you deeply
Breathing inside broken
Who are you?
I am tired
Pretty girl
Do not weep
While you sleep
Angry and sullen you
Demand, decry, wanting
Who am I?
Here, tonight
Dear sister
Say my name
Will you pray
All of these voices scream
Stealing pieces of me
Can you be
Satisfied
With just me?
Do you need
All to be
Powerful and mighty?
Change your mind will you please
Number one
Her name Sue
Dear brother
Call me Bill
I am you
Because of me inside

Mental Health

My demons I deny
One and two
I don't care
Who you are
Pulpit screams
This lost soul
Once upon a time
In my tortured mind

ABUSE

Roadkill

By Ndotono Waweru

Squeeze my wounds, drain their sorrows.
Ignite the train, forth to finite morrows.
Painted in blood, your roadkill awaits.
Floating in pain, life to abate.

Left in a grave, barely grieved.
Run over, by tires of wrath deceived.
Sprouted from the dead, freshly squeezed.
Feathers aglow, a crown unleashed.

Torture the words, make them speak.
Of your horrors, eras of terrors weak.
Cloaked in silence, you plied your fill.
Used and reused, fit for a landfill.

This is my symphony, charmed the odds.
Fixed my fate, shamed the lords.
Farmed my filth, famed my flock.
Wrath is not blind, oh what a shock!

Damage

By Thomas Spychalski

Dressed up for a beating,
Cringing at every movement,
Waiting for flesh hammers' reign,
Life becomes still, repressed.

Fear haunts as you wait again,
Hoping it will not catch you,
Something shuts down inside,
Hunted through deception of trust.

Bruises only show what will heal,
So many graves beneath my skin,
Exhumed at any point of threat,
Robbed of rational thought and action.

Existence in an unseen broken prison,
Sentenced for life, no jury in today,
Here is where the damaged reside,
On my flesh is where the mad man plays.

Fields Avenue

By Ayo Gutierrez

Welcome to the Pearl of the Orient Seas
We take pride in our sea, sun, and sand
for centuries . . .
The Spaniards
The Japanese
The Americans
came and conquered us
Exploited our
men
women
children
We drove them away
or at least we thought
for a sense of redemption
After our lands were converted into
a romping ground of restless tourists
on periodic trips to the archipelago
to eat, drink, and be merry
But we missed those days
of PX goods, yen and dollars
and deliverance from hell
they wanted to come back
and relive the glory days
on our free accord
When night falls,
our gloomy masquerade of the shanties
fades into the rambunctious party
Pulsating—
Balding men with bulging bellies
Cavorting
in a model's runway
gone berserk:
Gigolos and geishas
Young girls scantily clad in bikinis
Stilettoes clanking
Pole dancing
Pushing fragile bodies at perverse angles

Wearing garish make-up
to conceal their dread
for another taste of Sodom and Gomorrah
And
We offer our girls to these predators
Seeking sex for the price of a McDonald's burger and fries
or $10 to make them do anything
for pseudo marriage proposals
Arrests are seldom made
of the offenders
Because our tourism must thrive
despite economic turmoil
Because when you have nothing to feed your children
going back to the brothels
is the most scintillating offer
Everyday
we weep for the daughters of Eve
and sons of Adam
who meandered aimlessly
in the Garden of Eden
Met the serpent
Bit the apple
And drank the bitter waters of Marrah
When you come to the Pearl of the Orient Seas,
bask in the goodness of our sea, sun, and sand
But we do not have all the goodies you crave.
No, we do not have new prostitutes in the land.
We have already prostituted our people anew.

narrative (with caveats)

By Johnny Francis Wolf

: : :

tears she shed did make it worse, the more
he got annoyed . . . never will I write a verse
when truth I can avoid
battered, bruised and bandaged wife, tender
his intent . . . proof . . . the years she clung to life
her killing never meant
gentleman with every blow, black and blue
and red . . . benevolent, the chap I know
no wish to split her head
perhaps he had a drink or two, forgive him
for such thirst . . . taken from his point of view
the lady hit him first
blame him not his talent good for fist to
blister face . . . if alive the maiden would
admit she has no case
jury hearken, listen, learn, the woman begged
for more . . . pain did query, death did earn
this lowly, common whore

Overdose

By Kelly Glover

If you die from an overdose passed out in your car
People are going to be pissed
You'll never realize how much you would be missed
Your mother will find your body
Slack jawed and blue, slumped over the seat belt, eyes locked
open
Much to her horror, she will see how you have been coping
Your father will not be able to keep his family together
His drinking will increase, he couldn't handle the pressure
Your brothers and sisters will have such a heavy void
Their memories of you fading like old Polaroids
Your friends will remember when you weren't so fucked up
Some of them will likely join your early death club
Your enemies will break into your empty home with no
respect
These enemies are also your friends, but then again, what did
you expect?
When you decide to play in the dark
Your life is no longer a priceless piece of art
The pills, alcohol, cocaine, heroin, crack
All will leave you tied to a railroad track
Eat you alive from the inside out
Drugs want you have that permanent blackout
This death by drugs is an irrational disease
You will be reduced to ashes, dumped in a sea breeze
Some people would beg for the life you did not want
Your organs will live, the only life from your death
If you do not care about your life enough to not overdose
Think about the ones who do not want to see you
decompose

The Cocaine Lost

By M Lynn

Out of the cradle of filth
   Escaped with my life
Damaged and bruised
   But FAR from broken
Rose to challenge my demons
   And WON
Kindness was just a ruse
   No . . . I wasn't amused
Soul searching
   Swept away those doubts clean out
A Warrior Spirit

   Ready to battle
Take your shit no more
   Kicked the damn habit
But still carry the sword
   Double edged to sever its head
Another trophy for the wall
   Spit this poison out
The power of my pen
   Gives me strength
Defenses reinforced
   Wrote it out of my mind
And fucking killed it dead
   Sent it to Hell
Destroyed the root and
   OF THIS EVIL, I DO DEPART

Whore

By Tissy Taylor

Legs splayed
Eyes dead
Betrayed
Her cries
Un-wept
Her words
Unsaid
She is
Broken
Fucking whore
Addict slut
Needs her
Next score
It ain't real
Make believe
In her head
She matters
Fading
Craving
Her next fix
So she turns
Her next trick
I have a name
A home
A Mom
Someone's daughter
Not just fodder
Do you see me
When you use me
I'm abused
Like refuse
I'm garbage
Barraged with
False hope
Big dope
Arrest me

ABUSE

Detest me
Never free
Forsaken
I'm taken
To my grave
Now I lay me
Down to sleep
I pray the Lord
My soul to keep
Get your hands
Off me, you
Fucking creep
Stray from her path
Forgotten sheep

Whore

By Ndotono Waweru

Soaked in sin,
Painted lips puckered towards servitude.
Angular,
The sublime deity of desires.
Her heart broken to order.
Her death in every hissed moan.
A priced vessel of portals bereft.
Sensuous,
No haste nor waste as she commands
A rainbow to rupture over my colorless
Sky.

Anger accrued in heels.
Miles of trials.
Shame tucked 'neath her obedient mascara.
Ridicule trotted to pinnacle peaks.
Her virgin skill to prune lust
Perched on my frosted guilt.
Pleasant and plump
As she gently rearranges the moonlight.

She is a gatherer,
Of the roses life left unpetaled.
Nurtures them in a pod of regrets.
Renders ear to the musings of finless koi.
Flight to wingless kites.
Frozen heavens in her lips.
Her graves askew
In her symmetry of falsehoods.

Judy
By Kelly Glover

Judy is missing
Blonde hair blue eyes
Disappeared last week
But been gone a long time

Deep darkness took her over
She lived in her despair
All she needed was a flashlight
Her life now certainly in disrepair

Judy wanted to die
Naked and alone
No one to call
No love for her own

Judy dyed red
Too much makeup
To cover her sad
It was never enough

Those poison pellets
With that sugary venom
Were too sweet to resist
She aborts her life to them

Judy is missing
And is not coming back
She went to the Summit
And her life receded to black

No One's Child

By Tissy Taylor

It started simple
Daddy's star pupil
His favorite girl
Our own little world
All secrets and lies
I wanted to die

The noises I'd hear
The men who came here
Her body for blow
I was six years old
And only thirteen
When they came for me

At church, I would pray
For want of my pain
The priest turned to me
And I on my knees
A godly man's toy
Little altar boy

Of abuse and choice
A drug-addled voice
Living low, riding high
Barely surviving
All the same story
Whoring for money

With her legs widespread
Inside she is dead
Just another girl
This corner, this world
Is no one's child

Choices

By Jai Thoolen

When she first found she was pregnant,
Her whole world was torn apart.
Her mind was doing back-flips,
And those thoughts destroyed her heart.
That night kept playing over,
On repeat inside her mind.
He was ruthless. He was vicious.
It was rape of the worst kind.
There were threats and there was violence.
There was blood, bruises, and tears.
Those visions never fading,
And she'd live them all her years.
Her hardest life decision.
Should she keep a rapist's kid?
Impassioned moral choices,
And in the end, she did!
Her eyes first saw this baby,
And then horror flooded in.
A love like this must rally,
Because all she saw was HIM!

Daddy

By Lena Power

Daddy please don't touch me like you do
Mommy would be so upset if she knew
Don't make me feel like I am to blame
Don't put me through this horrible shame
I'm only nine, I don't understand why
You take my clothes off, even though I cry
Or force your fingers in between my legs
Even though for you to stop I beg
Why do you make me touch you there?
It's ugly, so wrinkled, hard to bear
Then when you force it up inside me
I bite my lip to quieten my agony
Tears of pain stream down my face
I feel so dirty, sordid, disgraced
You have taken away my innocence
Against your brutality I have no defence

You tell me I'd better keep my mouth shut
Or everyone will call me a little slut
You say Mom will think I lead you on
That if I talk all her love will be gone
For five years I was forced to endure
Your incestuous rape, leaving me unpure
Is it any wonder I failed all my grades
Living with a monster so depraved?
Finally I met someone who saw through
The hardened mask I wore because of you
She made me believe that I was worthy
When I accepted that truth I was finally free
I turned you down and saw you frown
In furious rage you tore away my gown
I screamed and my mother burst in the room
I'll be seeing you in court pretty soon.

Emotional Abuse

By Lena Power

Emotional abuse.
You never sought to harm me physically
Not wanting to leave marks for all to see
Instead you battered my mind, my heart
Sought to bring me down, tear me apart
Your words were bitter, so very cruel
My confidence you sought to overrule
You turned me from a confidant woman
Into a mouse, berated, downtrodden
Insidiously you invaded my mind
With sneers and comments, so unkind
Making me feel like I was a fake
That my aspirations I should forsake
When in public you were a gentleman
Giving others no reason to condemn
In private you raped me of all pride
Naked, exposed, nowhere to hide

Emotionally you were the death of me
Leaving deep scars no one could see
Stripping away all my self belief
Making me feel so incomplete

Why would you want to torture me?
Was your love just a fallacy?
Over time I became incapable
A puppet whose strings you pulled

Emotional abuse is a coward's crime
Just glad that I got out in time
Before I was crushed by your lies
You were immune to my heart's cries

You know, someday, you'll meet your match
The rewards of your sins you will catch
She'll tear you apart, turn you inside out
Leave you in pieces, of that I have no doubt.

Charlie in the Box

By Johnny Francis Wolf

Once upon a time there lived an odd, little whore named Charlie . . . who,
curiously, thought himself more a 'masseur.'
But most who knew him, and all who purchased his of-an-ilk ministrations,
understood just what he was, quite well. The only confused one was he.
Not that Johnny (of course I mean Charlie) wasn't driven by noble intent
... Especially true, when first pursuing his craft. But quickly discerned folks
were far more munificent, giving of alms and donations, when massages
were more, um . . . exotic.
Though Charlie loved women, 'twas men who most sought such service.

————

Attractively built, tall and athletic, strong jaw, not small in the 'talent'
department. But Charlie, naive, owned little of this. In his life, most often
dressed homeless . . . wearing old clothes, covered up good, hiding all
skin and bone. Quite a sharp contrast, to working with clients, completely
exposed, indeed fully nude.
Filled to the brim with fears, insecurities. Chockablock,
unrealized dreams . . .
An actor, too scared. A writer, not writing. An artist, no paper.
Believer, but no Church would have him.

————

Intuitive hands, compassionate heart, hurt not his business . . . as much as
the obvious, kept men returning. But unlike his friends, fellow Hollywood
hustlers, he turned away no one. Victims of stroke, vets without limbs,
cancer survivors, colostomy bags, obese, misshapen, quadriplegic, elderly,
frail, paralyzed, AIDS. Looking for love, they found the right place.
And yes, there were pretty ones. Treated the same.
We're ALL only steps 'way from broken.

————

He lived in the Land of Misfit Toys, thrilled to bring dwellers his measure
of joy. Felt blessed, could 'perform' with any and all.
A gift he was given, by God or whomever, to heal and be healed.
Untouchables touched.

————

But those wracked with guilt, the curious/married, were ever the hardest to slake. Deformities hidden, pain lying beneath, no curative stroke of his palm could reach their ache.

From giddy beginnings to making love middles, lasting through unhappy endings. Then dressed, money thrown, walked out the door. Heading for wives, children, home.

At the time of their leaving, the safe place he made . . . was now but reviled. If they could . . .

wouldst kill the messenger . . . their only lust left.

———

Charlie delivered the scroll with merely his touch, wordlessly reading the parchment. The truth was exposed, they already knew, how deeply it lived within.

Even his rehearsed debriefing for just such occasions . . . revulsion, repulsion, repugnance returned by the deaf.

They'd call to return, but a month to the day.

———

He helped who he could, letting go of the lost. Lived in his box, his eyes to the ground when stepping outside, knowing his place in the world.

Knew from the lessons he learned on the altar . . .

Boys such as he, were destined for hell.

Priests taught him well.

———

Prayers and love for Charlie and Mary (who bathed Jesus's feet). Angels be with you tonight.

And maybe 'tis Angels you are.

RELIGION

A Song for Leah

(For Leah Sharibu)
By Edentu Oroso

flip the primed pages of a pained heart
at the dusky borders of the absurd: feel your victory

a gaffe struck at the soul of a kingdom,
nothing would remain the same in this centre of gravity;

but a child, mirror of principled action you held up,
stared religion in the face, and revealed its starkness

brazen schemes you scorned by a force of will
a heroine in the narrative of unbridled terror

in the inversions that stands truth on its head
even with their chains, your lips chant freedom

Leah, faith's Amazon, daughter of Sharibu, history beckons:
Dapchi, the vaulted stage; your will, its wand of victory

your solitary tears in the crypt have become
oceans of yearnings to wrest the scenery of distress

everyone scurries in time to harvest the PVCs
in wait for the next pageant of votes

your voice resounds, the earth quakes, scripts unfurl
to etch the dawn with new paintings of the sublime

Leah, the proud Kingfisher who dares the strong winds
to fly stoically over the roiling rivers of being

with innocence and artistry over the elements,
stoking the memories of our collective impotence

in the drama of Chibok and the hand of Esau;
your strength has become our strength to remove the specks

threatening time after time to blind us into inaction;
for giving us hope in the face of odds, you've won the battle of life!

me too

By Johnny Francis Wolf

eat His body, drink His blood
hear the angels sing
lick the hand when dipped in mud
suck the bishop's ring
never let them see you wild
always show off well
never mind that priest with child
not your place to tell
heaven sent, this man of cloth
collateral the boy
swallow hallowed pastor's froth
f_ck the living toy

Puke Reverence

By Ayo Gutierrez

Holy Bible
Hundred Hedonists
High heels
You summon the windows of heaven;
for its drops to fall on hungry lips
Those nymphs of wealth
in their white robes and lofty heels;
Their purse and wallets
open like green smiles,
And they shout Amen to enslave simplicity!
They part their legs, as they draw you
into the orifice of their carnal cries
to receive your good omen
And their old folks
filling your stomach
with the finest fattening
A fitting arrangement
you told me
for them
to gain salvation
I never questioned a man of God.
You are one nebulous specter
of a charismatic leader,
circling like a circus
in a meaningless void
And gaining momentum in
this rollicking ride
of madness contagion
a beast put on a leash
under the cloak of modesty
And I've seen this beast
freed
a hundred times
its insatiable appetite
salivating
feeding

on youthfulness
and innocence . . .
But I would never question a man of God.
Tonight
we say our prayers together
and I drink in your sermon
in my white robes and high heels
Your simple fetishes:
this Holy Bible
hundred-dollar bills
and high heels
I say in one breath
in an upbeat march
as I cut you in three pieces
for desecrating
Cristina, Olivia, and Sarah
our dearest daughters
No need for a tomb and a grave;
The slain don't smile, speak or seek,
these effigies will burn
with you
the smoke and the fire
very much alive
celebrating your demise
while I break free
from your grasp
no longer the
spiritless slave to your caprice
I am the new God.
 . . . Or, the creator of design.

Body of Christ
By Ndotono Waweru

My child
In your blessed flock
I left
Yoked my faith to the Holy Ghost
Like a loyal servant
Your trinkets I chanted
Save
Under the Blood of Jesus
Christened and cleansed
Eucharist, Body of Christ my refuge
From the eternal fires of Hell
Your Hell on Earth
Your ornate pulpit of sin
Gospel ghouls in saintly robes
Shepherds anointed and ordained
Sacrifice of Calvary
Sacrifice in the rectory
Innocence
Robbed under the watchful eye
Of Mary Mother of Jesus
Your earthly hell
I ignored
A nave of hypocrisy
Pews upon pews of sacrificial
Lambs
Cardinals of cardinal sin
Investments of transgressions
Little angels
Defiled
Behold the folly of faith
Six feet under
He lies
And still bearing your cross
A bullet in his temple
And chaos in yours
For beneath your heavenly steeple

A predator hunts
Relish your final potluck, bishop
His suicide your homicide
Dust to dust, wrongs to wrongs
For thine is the kingdom
The power and the glory

By Pete Cox

So suddenly everything is offensive to read? To say?
To hear?
To speak?
People get all pensive and seethed and they spray it out of
their beaks with shrieks of disapproval and demand the
removal as it hurts their cuticles
As they command from the keys of destiny as they invest in
me and my blatancy of just being me
It's disgusting to these prisoners of sensitivity, then they
wave spirituality as actuality and dual over reality which is
testing my stability and my propensity for such heresy as the
fact is . . I'm just being me . . . a good old fashioned fuck off or
you will do or is that not spiritual enough for your ideal of
how to do this new age zeal?

And apparently I should've done this, shouldn't have done
that
Well how about everything after should is shit
Or should I have not even said that?
Just because you could doesn't mean you should
Well I should because I could before I wished I would but
should ruled would because it knew it could so maybe I
should or maybe even maybe's no good?

So who is this?
Is it you?
Or one of your many representatives?
All spiritual this and spiritual that
Spiritual kiss my spiritual crack
Spiritual is somehow now a spiritual trap
With spiritual shots fired from non-spiritual gats
The spiritual landed in the spiritual ego trap
So flap and tap with the this and thats

Suddenly life's no-shows become the Oshos?
And the biggest liar is now quoting Dr. Wayne Dyer! When
I've heard more truth come from Danny of the Dyer!

The fallen follies are now practicing Eckhart Tolle
On the other hand we got the master plan with his hustle
'stand that's Russell Brand with his 12-step scam and this
recovery dealing that's wrapped in healing and fancy feelings
for a bargain price that's apparently really not stealing from
the true meaning ??? . . . .

An impossible man with a possible heart and I thank you
hospital for all the jump starts that quickly followed with a
hasty depart
It seems wherever I go I leave a mark
As I'm more babestation than PlayStation still full of
frustration just debating which babe will let me inside her
station . . . Without all these sly-glanced indications of a date
timed destination of how long it takes to get in the gates like
heaven waits for my infestation to place allegations from
being a scallywag on a medication that still wags the skally in
a meditation . . . . . . this overly chronic poetic tonic is more on
it than sonic finding rings and tingz that make me grin all
over my skin and Ed Sheeran I don't believe you when you
sing it's not a ginger thing it's just a I call bullshit thing
When it's stuck my head it's sticky like glue
So I penetrate the paper with points of view
And assimilate joints of observant fruits
Instead of an interpretation of fluid loopy fruity hoops
To see and shoot which one best suits my insecure roots

And what's left is a window to the truth

Because I'm quite sensitive, so it's peppered in aggressive as
it's how I digest it until I dissect it and realise the whole
world can apparently cope without me??? Which was quite
absurd to see that I took myself so deliriously seriously and
was also a relief to let go of this grief as it ruled my boat . . it
was my captain and chief! A true belief that wreaked of
inevitable defeat yet once let go my heart shrieked in
disbelief and I discovered the ability to admit I'm flawed and
weak, which is true strength I can keep and reap

Disrupted by a disruptor
A virtuoso of virtual virtues conducts without structure, as a

conduit for a crafty conductor
Winding words for the wordplay wanderers' wonders
So, play along
Tune into the song
It'll switch quite often
See through the spectacles of a spectacular spectator, that
wants to debate the weight of time and space with ya
Time to direct the direction of a dictionary dictator, that
dictates the data from think to ink on paper in a form for all
to savor
It's a head full of words that are festering and pestering this
fledgling
Always thinking of ways of bending and transcending the
beginning and endings for pictures of words that require no
framing
Now I'm not blaming or saying this contention of word
tension and I didn't have the odd altercation from the
occasional frustration of spraying this Caucasian with too
much thought and contemplation was like surveying an alien
infestation
Now I just like conveying the messages and relaying the
relay marathon they want to keep playing
It's satisfying and gratifying so I'm going keep listening and
complying to what it's applying for I'm a trier at trying, I've
lied with the lying, bought with buying, blagged with
blagging, flown with the flying, cried with the crying and it's
guaranteed I'll die with the dying.

God-Skin

By Thomas Spychalski

I am your god today,
Welcome to the faithful,
I'll make sin wash away,
Bruises from the angels.

You are my subject now,
Never the flock shall leave,
If not I'll burn you down,
Now on your knees to pray.

Ritual, ritual,
Can you give me God-Skin?
Pestle, Pestle,
First I must grind you down.

I am the prophet they say,
Bringing bigotry and war,
I say it must be this way,
Heresy is but a new thorn.

You will obey the scripts,
Written in ancient fearing,
If not your soul is tipped,
I can heal it if you stay.

Preach, preach,
Can you lead to God-Skin?
Sin, sin,
Never shall you stray.

Verdict

By Ayo Gutierrez

She scans the crowd, eyes petrified
for in her accusers' calloused hands
are swiftly picked vindictive stones:
some damp and cold
like their beating hearts of contempt;
others sharp with briars
fashioned after the crown of thorns
forced upon the heads of them
whose temples are defiled or desecrated
according to their laws and letters
Hissing hypocrites with their
perfect remembrance of scarlet sins—
We live in the midst of broken men
unforgiven, hated, then forsaken
Their besmirched reputation,
souls bound in shackles
Claws of guilt boring
through their conscience
Deserted—
like lepers with worms
eating their rotten flesh . . .
Do they who cover their faces
in sackloth and ashes,
on the grounds prostrated—
receive a penance
for their trespasses?
...
Her body numbs, face crestfallen,
as the stones are released and
descend from the sky above her
Around her, the flames crack
and throw quivering shadows
of angry men who are determined
to send her to her grave:
either stoned to death
or burned in the pyre

Religious Hypocrites
By Lena Power

Look at all the sinners, heads bowed down in penitence
Begging god for absolution, how do they keep up their pretence?
Praying for their sins to be forgiven, asking for leniency
Dressed up in their Sunday best, smiling sanctimoniously

Eat the flesh of the Son, drink of the blood he shed
Receive the blessing of the cross on your hypocritical forehead
File out slowly one by one, with manners from your pews
Smiling and nodding to everyone, spreading the good news

Once the pleasantries are done, head for the local pub
Except the womenfolk of course, who must go prepare the grub
A few hours later, pockets empty, stagger through the front door
Your wife soon cowering in abject fear as you punch her to the floor

A normal occurrence in your eyes, one that she deserves
Her sin? Well, let's see, where to begin? Dinner wasn't served
Feeling a bit randy from too much booze you rape her violently
After all, all that she is good for is to serve your needs incessantly

Next door the wife is living the good life
An alcoholic prostitute in deep depression
You see, as a defenceless little girl she was taught a lesson
You are worthless, good for nothing, except to open your legs,
And that she was constantly made to do, no matter how she begged
The priest? Well he was being adequately entertained
By one of the choir boys whom he had asked to remain
Buggered if he was going to give up this sensation
He'd just confess his sins and receive consecration

Religious whores hiding behind a Sunday mask
Without even a conscience to be taken to task
Too totally oblivious to ever even own their own shame
After all is said and done, there's always the devil to blame.

god Not Capitalized

By Kelly Glover

When I asked god, Why is the sky blue?
The air quickly spun a black twister full of fiery electricity

I inquired to god, Why won't my flowers grow?
He sent a family of rabbits to devour my every bloom

Why didn't I get that new second job with the nice pay raise?
god promptly had me fired from the meager one I already had

I cried out to god, Why did I have a miscarriage?

I guess that wasn't enough, my entire uterus had to be removed

I asked god, Why did this happen?
He simply replied, Why not?

I asked god to heal my ailing grandmother
He did, but my parents died in a car wreck on the way to pick her up
from the hospital

I begged god, Please take away this horror in my bowels
He gave me Crohn's disease which is forever pain

I asked god, Can you send me the man of my dreams?
Instead I found myself raped in my nightmares

Please kill me! I pleaded with god
I have just celebrated my 103rd birthday

I tested god, Am I on the right track?
He opened up sinkholes blocking either direction

I asked god, Why do people find peace in your belief?
Religious wars forever infest this planet

I quizzed god, How do I find Satan?
He said, You're talking to him! Nice to meet you

I asked god, Why should I believe in you?
god said nothing

Jesus Never Was

By Kelly Glover

If Jesus were alive today
Would he do it all the same?
Give up his existence for humanity
Would he take all of our blame?

For famine and for war
With the good comes the bad
Granting woeful wishes
As if that's all he has

If God were to show his face today
Would he again crucify his only son?
Eager to cause suffering by his choosing
Still be forced to spill his own flesh and blood?

Jesus never was
A messiah or a deity
Maybe he was a nice guy
False idol though he must be

Take blame for your own actions
Sins or whatever you like to call them
Don't expect a fairy tale
To solve all your trivial problems

Denial

By M Lynn

Stolen innocence
    Discarded and tarnished
Misplaced violence
    Fighting this fucking Hell within
Drown in my own blood and tears
    Floods of memories and tastes of sins
Tried to cut it out of me and kill this damn silence
    Prayers unheard; no salvation awaits
Knocked at Death's door
    Turned away more than once
Hell isn't ready for me yet and
    St. Peter has locked Heaven's gates

The Gospel of the Poor

By Ayo Gutierrez

I was a wee lass when I first heard
a sermon preached by a Dominican priest
In a parish adorned with
candelabras casting shadows
of the most elaborate graven images
While we town folks clothed in muddy slippers,
our backs scorched in the fields
We waited fervently for our turn of communion
for the remission of our sins
"Blessed are the poor, for theirs is the kingdom of heaven," said Father
If we expect a year of harvest and bounty
Father must keep us in the flock
Father needs our tithes and offerings
We must not hold back a single penny
even a widow's mite
Beatus es pauperis
The ground is cursed for our sakes
we learned one Sunday School afternoon
So we are left to pick our poison
From our scanty proportions
Partakers of misery and woes
Vessels agog with false hopes
Predisposed to follow our well-greased politicians
and salivate after their pork barrels
Who buy our votes for a bag of rice and sardines
They toss our squatters here and there
and we bear our children everywhere
Father taught us to multiply and replenish the Earth
and take no thought of the morrow
Bienaventurados los pobres
When we scan the front pages of our newspapers
Thousands of jobs await us,
a greener pasture in the land of the voyeurs
Let us send our women to be housemaids and prostitutes
Forget about the verdure of our lands
Soon, the capitalists will come

for the plunder of our resources
The government will take care of us so why bother?
Beati I poveri
The corruption of the doctrines
The proliferation of dogmas
The debauchery of the Heaven-seekers
We know so much—and yet,
we also know so little.
The plight of the hungry and the homeless
We have become fools
to romanticize our debacles
Blessed are the poor
For when our last morsel of food
drops on the ground
And Heaven's doors swing open to receive
its faithful acolytes
We have a long tale to tell
An eternal confession
of our sufferings in the flesh
Because we listened to Father

On This Rock

By Lena Power

Every day in the golden cathedral
The plate is passed for offerings
The Bishop wears his lavish regalia
While the common people are suffering
Poor and homeless begging for bread
While the altar is adorned with gold
Dreams of redemption in the eyes
Of those whose sins remain untold
Children shiver in tattered rags
While the higher order ever feast
Preaching that if you turn to god
You will be saved from the beast
Who is the true beast here, I ask
Hoarding riches whilst innocents suffer?
Ever through the ages the church keeps all
Preaching to us to share with each other

Fingers adorned with precious stones
All of which could help the needy
In sanctimonious pride withheld
Ever adding to the riches of the greedy
 "Open up your eyes to god" they say
 "For ye are his precious children"
So precious the echelons let you die
Believing in brainwashed illusion
 "Upon this rock I build my church
Go forth and preach my teachings"
Jesus fed the hungry, did he not?
His compassion for all far-reaching
His church became organised crime
To overrule and keep all glory
With the doctrines of man instigated
Deliberately corrupting the true story.

In His Name

By Tissy Taylor

Catholic girl on her knees
Praying for his release
Begging God let her be
Punished for sins bequeathed

In the name of Father
Gentle waters calm her
For wings offers prayers
Beneath she disappears

Wooden crosses aglow
Hooded figures below
Cry to release his soul
Spilling red on Earth's floor

Forgive me all my sins
These beads to pay my rent
Lurks this evil within
Washed in waters christened

His scripture etched in stone
Rise from this bloody tomb
Pledging tithes to heal wounds
The whores who pimp His word

Sinner

By Tissy Taylor

Wear me across your chest
Breathe me in
Flailing limbs
Beat my heart
Exposed sins
Chastise
Repent
You shall seek (me)
In the End
The Devil lives in us
He prays for our demise
And still you let him in
Dastardly
Bastard
You want what you can't have
Tempt and tease her
Arouse her wild
Seek freedom in
Naivety
This girl wants
What she wants
Temptress Queen
Fated heart
She gives
She bleeds
Ripped open
Stem and tide
Wash away
Derision
Extinction
Left behind
Honour you
Thy Mother
Thy Father
Rejoice world
Multiply

Jesus Christ
Our savior
Manipulates
Who I am
All these rules
I can't abide
God-damned choice
Makes me decide
No miracle
Simply life

REVOLUTION, VIOLENCE, AND WAR

Soldier's Prayer

By Tissy Taylor

Let me lay my body down
For to rest your weary head
On pillows, stone and mortar
Earthen soils do make my bed

Let me weep o'er my brother
For to harvest your bounty
Crush the bones, my savage mind
Your feast this land of plenty

Let me pray this life I give
For to speak and claim your Faith
A simple cross to mark my grave
Etched in stone, freedom my name

Let me lay my body down
For death has claimed us all
My eyes no longer seeing
How mighty is our fallen?

Beat the drum

By Tissy Taylor

A feather flag high on a post
Ripples of colour taking flight
Hastened in winds changed o'er time
Red stained lines spilling into white
Sing a keen, the mourners lost prayer
To honour and to remember
Sacrificed lamb, his soul slaughtered
Breathless in grounds deep 'neath the sun
New life shrouds those buried in wait
Though we carry your memory
Faded is the weight of your arm
The sound of your voice a whisper
On whims and larks we must soldier
Police a world unfamiliar
For sake of peace, ne'er to return

A General's Mirror
By Ndotono Waweru

I have looked through the tatters of life.
Deeper into the cavities of evil.
I have seen the breath of mountains
Choke the orphans who beg at her feet.
I have looked into foolish mirrors.
Seen a hero in my reflection.
Distorted faces without identity.
The darkness held behind my name tag.
I have rummaged through faith and found
Nothing of value.
Ashes and dust and shadows of the
Humans we were.
I have heard dawn beg dusk back.
Seen the tears of children with missing eyes.
Vultures feasting on failing flesh,
Nourishing the greedy god of war.
I have tasted the rich agony of death.
Mothers willing the breath to flee
Their mangled darlings.
Deafening screams devoid of sound.
I have dined with corruption.
Made a case to kill out of greed.
My gold walls my golden medals.
Souvenirs of the void I have become.

--

By Pete Cox

War is business
People are the currency
Keep the numbers balanced
Destroy a collective sanity
To feed a few's depravity
Warlords using us to model their next big score
Spray it over the news
Clock up those views
Keep us glued, try and protest
It won't stop what they do
Then sell us remembrance
In parades of elegance
We see through this negligence
Use a God to bless your mess
Convince a nation it's a biblical test

OPPRESSIVE FAMILY TRADITIONS

Prisoners

By Kelly Glover

Since Daddy went to prison
Things just ain't been the same
Too many drug deals caught up
Long time 'fore we see him again

For a while Momma and Grandpaw
Took care of me and my sister
'til Momma got pregnant with Grandpaw's kid
An my inbred brother came into the picture

Since Daddy done been gone so long
Momma found her a new boyfriend, John Thomas
He liked to check my panties to make sure they were clean
And look in all my holes for stuff he wanted to see

Momma worshipped her new-found man
Like Jesus done returned
She wore more blue eye makeup
One of the many tricks she learned

She hid his hits with sunglasses
Cigarette burns on eyelids
Singed her long lashes
He watched everything she did

She cooked and cleaned but it was never enough
John Thomas always wanted what she didn't give
Momma tried to make him happy everything she did
But he just made her feel like she didn't wanna live

At night when Momma finished her wine
Started snoring watching the T.V.
I pretended to sleep deep
When John Thomas came to see me
He would make his fingers disappear
In the caverns of my body

He said, "That's where the good juice is"
As he stuck his tongue inside me

The years flew by with Daddy in the pen
Momma got so angry, abused, and depressed
She found it hard to get up and get dressed
The pills she took left her a sloppy mess

Took care of my younger sis and cousins
John Thomas used my lil' baby brother
As his favorite moving target
Hittin' the boy every day, one right after another

Except one day he hit him too hard
Brother started shakin'
Teeth chatterin' eyes buggin' out
I couldn't get him to wakin'

John Thomas didn't care
But he musta been pretty worried
'cuz he dumped the boy in the river
After cutting him to pieces in a hurry

Then John took my mom and sis
Guess he forgot about me
Put a bullet under each of their chins
Blows his own brains out finishing the evil deed

Now Daddy's lil' girl is all growed up
Found myself my very own man
That likes to bruise my thighs and black my eyes
I just wanna make him happy as I can

God Gave Me

By Tissy Taylor

Eyes that I may witness beauty
Ears that I may listen
Arms to embrace fear
Legs for to carry me forward
Still I am shrouded in black cloth
Wrapped in linen masking His gifts
Through your lens I see
In your voice I speak
Escape my wiles, teach me to fish
Take my will, my mind, my pleasures
Invisible chains
To which I am bound
Forsaken is potential
Buried hope, dreams unrealized
I have no freedom
I beg for mercy
Why must my voice shout in whispers
Linger I in the darkest corners
Release these chains and
Let her reach the stars
Give her wings to fly and to soar
Heed the prayers that go unanswered

Your Little Whore

By Jai Thoolen

"I needed the money," she said,
"I get paid for just doling out head.
I drive a nice car these days too.
It's all I have got I can do.

Don't judge when you don't even know.
I didn't have elsewhere to go.
My Daddy loved me the wrong way.
And now, like the others, he'll pay.
My mother claims she never saw.
Be proud, Mum, of your little whore!"

"School was a waste of my life.
I don't wanna be somebody's wife.
I just need to be paid for my skill.
Those things SHE won't do? Well, I will!
You wanna get bang for your buck?
Well, money up front and we'll fuck!

I'm cleaner than most, take a chance.
No condom is extra, let's dance!
I get a new 'boss' every hour.
But I'm the one wielding the power."

"Plenty of men, plenty of cash.
The Pill and a cream for that little rash."

"Don't you dare even talk about dignity.
Does it matter? Do you think YOU have any?"

Succumb

By Ndotono Waweru

She adorns your hunger
With crumpled silence.
Her foreign innocence cold.
Unripe!
Living on stolen childhood.
Dying of borrowed puberty.
A flower purloined from the
Cradle.
On the table of your yawns,
She starves.
Drying in a vase
Unloved.
Unwatered curiosity in a desert of
Choices.
A victim of your ailing
Vanity.
She is
Your blindfold to a past
Dethroned.
Your pathway to a future
Deboned.
You moan foregone sunsets
In her groans.
Minnowed bait in your panic
To subdue a recycled
Youth.
When reckoned she
Smiles.
When beckoned she
Dies.
Succumbs
To her unrelenting
Reality.

Train To Glory

By M Lynn

With a wolf's smile
They invite us in
To sign the bottom line
Voluntarily gift them our life
To defend the lives of others

Sent to camp with sheep
Of all kinds to mill around
Got our attention by
Barking our flaws in our faces
Gutting our souls
To see who will break

Groomed like camouflaged robots
Trained to survive and to kill
March to one beat
Keeping it simple and neat
Follow the leader
Wash the brains
In Federal Government blood

POLITICS

Delicadeza

By Ayo Gutierrez

Don't get me started
About how this word has changed
Profoundly
In regard to effective governance
Spouses
Children
In-laws
Grandchildren
Time ticks in decades
As each takes their turn
In public positions
Honor redefined
Or misplaced
Padded receipts
Cheating beneath the table
Politicians—a nefarious ensemble
Singing lies through sharp-toothed smiles
A lullaby for our economy's demise
Graft
Corruption
Endless extortion
A shameless parade of sickness
Passing for reputation
No regard for the masses
Laden as they are with taxes
Official car
Official mansion
Official budget:
One for all, all for one
A royal feast
Bountifully shared
Among the few
Private firms and foundations
Siphoned by greedy spouses
When discovered, they abscond, retract
And don faked injuries

Politics

Then, hands washed, lawsuits evaded
They hibernate
In their Beverly Hills-inspired estates
Oh, the myriad ways they bend the laws!
Power corrupts, power overflows
Power they glean
Freshen their face with it
To appear clean

Ugh
Need I say more?

This Farmland

By Edentu Oroso

This sprawling farmland –

like strokes etched deep in the womb of the sun
uniquely spread over the boulders of the moon
watched by the tender arms of the stars:

Did you not marvel at its expanse and beauty
with enlivened thoughts about its fecundity?

This verdant farmland –

of rustling corn-fields and swaying rice stalks
and the ever-brilliant tint of pregnant tubers
bulging forth from the livid veins of the earth:

Were we not blest to be so hosted in paradise
with its cache of bounties and experience?

This great farmland –

tinged with long history of hydrocarbons
stacked in the bowels beneath corn and rice fields
and in the deep cauldrons of the Atlantic:

Did we not chant 'hosanna' to the barrels
of the earth's blood that fed our naked desires?

But this quaking farmland –

that sends birds and rodents scampering afield
into their nets and burrows
for fear of thunder's clap
and the torrent of wasteful rain:

Would our corn-fields still sway with zest and life?

Politics

And this endless lightning —

that so blinds the harvesters from sowing
the seeds for tomorrow's great seed
that makes them sink under the weight of harvest:

Is that the lot of this farmland?

Pen of Wise Pigs

By Edentu Oroso

Graft's but an art when the craft
is mastered in the putrid pen of wise pigs;
Graft's but graft when fevered fools
indulge themselves after the ways of pigs' pen.

The pig that wields the might is but king
in the jungle of beastly canter;
The fool that imagines self as pageant pig
reckons not with the unfair banter of life's camels.

Who Are You to Decide?

By Tissy Taylor

Who are you to decide
What is best for me?
Everything I do
For my family
About them
About me
No pretending
Or wondering
Who do I believe?
What is left or right
Hidden or make-believe
Tell me the truth
And let me see
What I need to
Make decisions
What is best for me
Is what you feed me
your version of truth
Hidden agenda
Make it right and
Gimme, gimme
Feed your poor and
Feed your hungry
Help for the mental
The rich and needy
Money for black
Money for white
Build your wall
It's your call
But I am telling you
My money goes so far
Help me, will you?
Show me the way
Give me the entire verse
Not the Hollywood story
All your bullshit
It ain't enough

I am tired
I am done
Middle class dollars
Buy only so much
I like my health care
I like my free stuff
You slam your leader
It is all his fault
Yet you vote
Who's the clown?
Someone is voting
For the guy in charge

Dancing Skeletons

By Kelly Glover

Republicans, Democrats, and Liberals
Elephants, Donkeys, and Pigs
Old white men
Telling lies

Fake news, scandals, and harassment
Our leaders all have skeletons
Dancing in their closets
Begging to be addressed

Voters, Constituents, and Deciders
Tricked into believing they count
No matter what their choice is
It's all worth the same amount

Our leaders are the most guilty
Yet blame they will never see
Lies spew like vomit with the flu
Peasants and paupers me and you

A Migrant's Migraine

By Ndotono Waweru

From colourful cracks they sprout.
Rise from flaming pyres
To claim trophies made of dust.
Crumbs of liberty and lavish
Packaged and sold
By the glamor of Hollywood.
Democracy flavored servitude
For dreamers of
Freedom.

Like pottery from the kiln,
They break.
Their fated realities walled in milk and
Honey.

Twilight stilettos.
Wares in thongs, thrusts survived.
Land tilled, floors tiled.
Vineyards picked at the crack of dawn.
Last night's seeds laundered from
Linens of sins.
Toilets clogged with gluttony
Plunged.
Kids nursed while lawns get
Their weekly manicure.
Dresses tailored, drywall installed.
Tacos and tofu,
Life is good!

From our Faraday cages
We watch this churn.
Charm guilt to submission with
Lopsided grins and memorized
Poise.
After all,
We are but aliens in
Cultural casks sadly

Fermenting into
Humans.

Western World View

By Thomas Spychalski

Out here in the Western world, Poverty combines with shame.
A tool of segregation,
Broken freedom nations,
The empty promises here that we are the same.

Not enough that we rape the outside world,
We must pull our own mothers and daughters down too,
Land of plenty,
With stomachs empty,
Because payment to the masters is always due.

If you ride the paved, lined roads,
Across the lands of fruitful harvest,
As you will roam,
You'll see some without a home,
The ones the road hits the hardest.

At the tops of the hills and mined mountains,
In mansions and opulence of church and state,
You'll see the slave drivers,
Chess game, the pawns and compilers,
Different breed that only gives out what profits and what is minimally
required.

Carving dividing lines between the haves and have nots,
Ladders you can ascend at the price of your soul,
If you play the game,
A slave the same,
But one who produces what they stole.

One last paint stroke of the diminished human masses,
Living in shadow in the caverns of burning lights,
He is starving and frozen,
Oh yes somebody owes him,
On the killing floors of freedom resides his plight.

Under Cover
By Tissy Taylor

A few careless words
To the world at large
Spouting my wisdom
Half-cocked and deluged
Clever little girl
Drunken pedestal
Wants to scream and shout
Tell you what is real
Pseudo is my 'nym'
Pulpit preach a game
Repression of my,
Expression is not
In the equation
Rather I sit in
Judgement, while spewing
Sanctimonious
Truth. Crapping on your
Constitution.
Twitter reporter
Interested supporter
Social media
Platform of false news
Rise from the shadow
Trolls lurking, after
Every misstep
Beg you to falter
I have to wonder
If I should blunder
I shall earn my own
Hashtag result!

Protection

By Simon Jackson

In the judicial chambers at Tooting Magistrate Court, the Magistrate, a weathered old man, peered up at us with tired eyes.

"Thomas James Atkins and Lucy Michelle Atkins," he looked down and read from a document, "you have both been found guilty of the charge of child negligence, contravening the Child and Families Act, amended 2034." He scanned some notes that lay on his broad, lacquered desk, and then leaned back in his chair, looking at each of us in turn. He removed his glasses, wiped his palm down his face, and let out a sigh.

"Mr. Atkins, you told the court that your son had grown out of his previous safe-hat and that you couldn't afford a replacement. Yet, there are many government financing options available for safety clothes, for which very few people are ineligible. I understand that your local council even provides grants for families in particularly difficult circumstances." He leaned back. "On top of that, your history of civil disobedience, for which you've been before this court a number of times, makes your story, well, unconvincing," he raised one eyebrow.

"Mr. Atkins. I wonder, did you attend the Kindermoord marches?" I looked up. "Oh, don't worry, you needn't to answer any questions at this stage, but you remember what happened? I recall it was one of those rare occasions when protest prompted real action. Doubtless, there was already recognition amongst legislators of the urban traffic problem, but still, the protests hammered it home. And the 2034 amendment reversed the trend overnight. Child traffic deaths reduced by half. Now, it is within your rights to protest any issue you see fit. But please remember that there are lawful ways to do it, and for God's sake, Mr. Atkins," he glared at me, "leave your child out of it."

He replaced his spectacles and rearranged some papers on his desk. He wrote some details on some documents and Lucy and I signed our conviction notices.

Mitcham Road was a wall of moving traffic that hissed on the wet road as it sped by. An oily haze hung over the vehicles and filthy rain smeared the buildings and the crowds. From the steps of the courts I looked towards Tooting, but saw only distant shadows fade into the smog. I pulled out my mobile.

Lucy fussed over Robert, looping his filter mask over his brand-new white safe-hat. He tugged at the straps.

I raised my voice above the volume of the street, "There's plenty of bus stops just past Broadway. It's only ten minutes."

A densely packed stream of people swept along the narrow pavement— single-file in each direction. A gap opened in the flow of people. We slipped across the pavement and joined the kerb-side file, matching our pace to the other pedestrians. Lucy led Robert and then me.
Robert looked up at the passing faces of the people heading towards Mitcham—distracted like any four-year-old. I placed my hand on his safe-hat and turned his head so that he watched the pavement ahead.

As we passed Broadway Underground Station, the flow of people changed. The inevitable chaos at the station's multiple exits diverted us to relative shelter against the buildings, and then back to edge of the pavement, again within arms-reach of the speeding traffic.

I heard a sharp shout behind me and turned my head, struggling to see while maintaining my pace. From the corner of my eye I saw Robert also look and I turned back, "Please, Robbie, eyes ahead . . ." I felt a hard shove from behind and I stumbled into Robert. He tripped and tilted sideways off the kerb. My hand shot out and grabbed his arm. Still falling, my other hand slapped onto the wet road and caught us, crouched over the gutter, the noise and spray from the traffic in our faces.

I glanced up and saw a lanky youth, running and swinging a briefcase like a machete, dashing the people aside and shouting threats. He quickly vanished into the crowd. An old man in a business suit, out of breath and with his face twisted in shock, watched him go.

I lifted Robert back onto the pavement and looked him over. "You okay, little fella?" He wiped his eyes and nodded.

The crowd, like water, flowed instantly around us as we huddled by the kerb. Lucy double-checked Robbie and a tall gent caught my eye.

Evidently, he had seen us fall and patted Robert on his safe-hat as he walked by, nodding solemn approval of our parental precautions.

It was a half-hour wait for the bus. On board, Robbie fell asleep and Lucy and I took turns to carry him. There were only four seats on the bus, but near Wandsworth, one became free and Lucy sat with Robbie curled up on her lap.

As we stepped off the bus at Roehampton, the darkened sky had vanished behind the grimy fog which glowed orange from the sodium street lights. The rain fell heavier then, and I struggled to pull Robbie's' hood over his safe-hat. Doing so just tilted his head back, and then it rained in his eyes and soaked his filter mask. Lucy pulled back the hood and handed him our only umbrella.

Fluorescent light spilled through the barred doorway of the store and reflected off the wet concrete path. "Hold my bag please, sweetheart, I don't want to mess around with the security guard." Lucy and Robert waited outside and, after a short queue outside and a trouble-free security check, I bought bread and milk. I also found a tin of tuna hidden behind the soft drinks (which never appeared out-of-stock), so at least we'd get some protein, though it emptied my pockets until payday.

As I left the bright lights of the shop, I saw Lucy and Robbie standing across the road, sheltering under a tree. As I drew near, I heard Robbie's sobbing and Lucy called out, tears in her voice, "Tom. Tom, they took it."

I rushed towards them and she glanced down into the dark part of Danebury Avenue, away from the shops and buses, where the street lights were no longer used. There, two dark figures sprinted towards the shadows; one held my bag and the other swung Robbie's white safe-hat. Too far to catch up, I stood helpless in the rain and watched them slip into the night.

OPEN THEMES

Voices

By Tissy Taylor

One hundred footsteps in a room
Glass walls lay bare my hidden self
With hands cupped in solemn prayer
She heeds the voices in her head

Trapped within the dark of mind
Seeking truth from her unraveling
Soothe the warrior, cage the beast
Fierce trumpet the madness they bring

Weep solemn, desperate for light
Preen beneath sun-kissed azure sky
Cleaving despair, demanding breath
Only wanting to feel alive

One hundred footsteps in a room
Uncertain if two are her own
Music echoes breaking silence
Dancing to see her shadow move

V Monologue

By Ayo Gutierrez

The things you expect of us
are not your humdrum task
when you ask for a dozen children
you simply don't chide
consider our yearly wear and tear
when you ask for an Alistair
surely you don't mistake us for a concessionaire?
or a factory filled with assembly lines
of body parts to stitch on a daily grind
we are not created from rubber
a tear so deep and wide is a nightmare
those weeks of leaks are morbid
oft times my plea is for this pee to flee
a day this scourge will set me free
could we cope with a wound infection
brought about by a C-section?
could we not cope with faecal malady
from a bad vaginal delivery?
in the tangled web of Roman justice
on to centuries of hapless guesses
evidence is mounting fast
of mothers and fetal deaths
the danger of childbirth
is a Pandora's box

Working women must resume work
after a few months of pseudo rest
we are like Atlas who carries the world
be a super mom and do our best
why, the dog has more time to heal
for years our offspring rely on us for meals
they mumble and they cripple
little vampires sucking our nipples
whilst our wound below is bloody and fresh
you make your nightly advances
to you whose ignorance we must endure
we recite our litany of woes

we take our dose
of Aspirin and Heparin
Pytocin and Oxytocin
trust us when we claim
we have learned the art of inflicting pain
when we are taken to the delivery room
after hours of laborious labor
it doesn't matter if our legs are parted wide
hoisted in a cold metallic apparatus
how many times have we farted loud
in the course of transvaginal ambush?

If you see our children misbehaving
never throw us your killer glance
you know nothing about our suffering
please spare us your askance
mind the things you expect of us!

Home

By Johnny Francis Wolf

he left the commonplace
with aimless moving forth
more lines upon his face
and snowy hairs up north

met with others scorned
whose only sin was art

writers unadorned
their wallets filled with heart

and with these no-good louts
of fading skin and bone

unknown their whereabouts
but nevermore alone

- - -

By Pete Cox

A formation of fortitude holds me in my solitude
I talk a form of truth yet question the source's roots
Disguised in a healthy suit is a tarpit of dark wealthy fruits
Nailed to an omen I speak a light-bound sermon
Mind won't close because the bars always open
A gentleman who can be well spoken spits violence because it surges
through his totem
Holding onto lonely through arms stretched openly
I ask why the supernatural chose me?
Naturally I long to be but a habitat's habits are holding the keys,
formatting gaps in an earthbound trap
Sometimes I'd like to wind it back and edit this track
So I study the facts with a fictional map
A mystical mind bound on galactic adventures
Searching for someone to share the treasure
Universal dustman blowing fallen stars in the path of those who play
with wrath while soaking in a wormhole bath
Finding the ugly beautiful because in school my eyes were the only pupil
Searching for freedom while finding containment
I never signed the paper agreeing to this arrangement

Dark Horse

By Tissy Taylor

This dark horse
Forever
She is lost
Led astray
Sinners pray
Find their way
False claims
Judgement day
Holy grail
God's labyrinth

Wicked games
Shameful ways
Innocence
Takes my place
Blood is spilled
Against her
Broken will
Shattered is
False promise
Wilted, worn
She is torn
Asunder
Start anew
Please save her

On one knee
Silently
Pew and plea
Darling child
Lost in wild
Surviving
All she knows
To keep sane
Intended
Descendant

Fresh her pain
Wiped clean
New face and
A new name
Restless girl
Bewildered
Grey cinder

Dark horse your
Tricks and trysts
Flawed remiss
Seeking truths
Forgiveness
Haunted youth
Used vessel
Altar-ed sin
Impassioned
Suicide
Waging war
Wanting more
Hide her eyes
Shield the pain
Valley girl
Laying still
Nothing left
A dark shell

By Pete Cox

The purse of perception is changing direction
My procedure might proceed the known done deeds of certain beliefs
So I'll engage my rocket feet for a hasty retreat
Swim on the moon in lunar seas, lunar tickled treat
Where the lunatics cast tidal showers
to remind humans, that they
don't hold all the power

Swiping planets for dates,
because Venus is planning a
nebula break
So I'll surf around Saturn's
rings
See what the sixth planet is
saying

I feel the shirk after Mercury
merked Earth
Venus got between us and it
kicked up some stardust
Mars got testy and all
This is what happens
when you're keeping it
terrestrial

I keep the mind open
So I hot-footed across to the
Jovians
Now Neptune had the
fortune of gas balloons
Jupiter jested with Uranus
and the party got a bit
heinous
Got a butane burn whilst
skanking on Saturn
On these party planets
anything can happen

Set on a rehabilitation course
I stumble upon a dwarf
Pluto is where all the space
degenerates go when they've
run out galactic dough
After a service
I must be leaving
More planets
I am seeking
This what happens in a moment
whilst I'm daydreaming

ABOUT THE AUTHORS

Pete Cox is from Slough, England. He hosts an open mic night called The Innerverse and runs the YouTube channel Typical Pete. He writes based on experiences, annoyances, and just about anything. He writes a poem a day.

Kelly Glover is a thirty-something-year-old single mother from Greensboro, NC. She is the fearless leader of three kids, two cats, and one failed marriage. Her work can be found in various online journals and anthologies and her first book of poetry, *The Light of my Dark*, is available on Amazon.

Ayo Gutierrez pens her art in the Philippines. Gutierrez's poetry collection *Yearnings* showcases her latest work—while also featuring poems by an international cast of eighteen different writers in an array of poetic styles. Ayo's poetry has appeared in different anthologies: *I Have a Name: Anthology of Prose and Poems on Mental Disorders* (2017); *Hidden Constellation* magazine (2017); *A Promise of Doves* (December 2018); and *Transcendence: The Anthology of Human Thought* from Trode Publications (February 2019). She also co-authored *Bards from the Far East: Anthology of Haiku and Kindred Verses*. She also runs a local tv show called Travel Art TV.

Simon Jackson lives with his wife and two children in South London where he works for the direct benefit of humankind, and also as a sports physiologist. In recent years, an overwhelming desire to tell others what to do has compelled Simon to write stories and poems consisting of dark speculation. *In the Crosshairs* is Simon's debut publication.

M Lynn was born in Paulding, Ohio. She left for the Air Force right after high school for five years. M has been writing since age fourteen and it has been her mentally therapeutic release for many years.

Edentu D. Oroso is a biographer, poet, essayist, magazine columnist, novelist, and public speaker. He's the author of *Tears from a Rose*; *The Alfa Sky*, a biography of Air Marshal Ibrahim Mahmud Alfa, Nigeria's longest-serving Chief of Air Staff; *Wings of Freedom*, a biography of Ralph Igbago, former Deputy Speaker Benue State House of Assembly, Nigeria; and *Songs of the Gilded Pen* under the pen name Dean Max.

Lena Power is a retired course coordinator, trainer, coach, and facilitator for London Underground Ltd. currently living in London, U.K. She began writing poetry at about the age of ten after the death of her grandmother, but did not continue. She restarted approximately two years ago after a breakdown, and poetry is now her passion and lifeline. Lena belongs to several poetry groups, and many of her works have been published in several anthologies produced by Poetry Planet. She has received many certificates of excellence and merit for her published poetry. She has her own page, "Enter my World," and is looking ahead to publishing her own poetry collection.

Thomas Spychalski has written for various online and offline publications since 2006 including *Kasterborous*, *Whotopia*, the 2011 book *Ultimate Regeneration*, and *City to Country* magazine.

Additionally, he worked as a reporter in Texas and still writes a column remotely for the same newspaper for the past six years.

Tissy Taylor began writing as soon as she could hold a crayon. From Ontario, Canada, she found her writing voice early on, serving two community newspapers for several years. She currently works as a Senior Business Analyst/Communications Manager for GM and recently released her first poetry collection entitled *Madness, Chaos Unraveled*.

Jai Thoolen is a diverse author from Australia. Children's books, including *My Beard*, are the main focus of his work. He has a need to get words out at all times and does so in many forms of poetry and short stories (or 'yarns' as they're known in Oz). Oftentimes, there is a cheeky or fun streak in his writing, though he does have a serious and maybe even sinister side.

Ndotono Waweru is a published poet from Kenya with a love for imagery and the talent to make it visible. He treasures simplicity and fluidity in abstract poetry. He is a believer in the mobility of words.

Johnny Francis Wolf is a former actor and model. He currently lives in the high desert, three hours north of Los Angeles. He writes daily poems on his Facebook author page "Daily Poem." His most cherished work is his script entitled *Jelly Donuts*, which he hopes to land on a movie contract soon.

ABOUT THE ARTISTS

Emily St. Marie is a West Coast artist and children's book illustrator. She does her line-work with an old quill pen, swipes acrylic on canvas with a palette knife and boar's hair brushes, and explores the depths of color, shade, and light using an ancient set of oil paints. Emily loves portraits, nature, animals, and "cartoon-realism." She is currently working on an Art Nouveau, medieval-inspired, graphic novel called *The Moon Goddess*, and a collection of fairy tales.

Jinque Romanban-Dolojan is an organic farmer, poet, writer, and graphic designer who loves geeking out for book cover designs and writing poems in pitch-black or gothic imagery. Her recent illustration was for the book *An Arabian Adventure* by David Wagoner. She authored *Hue Wins?* and *Someone Painted the World Black* and co-authored *Plethora of Poetry* and *Tanka & Tan(g)ka*. When not making her hands dirty with paints, watercolors, or soil (for planting crops of course!), she loves staring at the sky while patiently praying for moon dust and stardust to envelope her with the universe's exquisite brand of magic.

Printed in Great Britain
by Amazon